WHAT IS HALLOWEEN?

I Like Holidays!

Elaine Landau

Enslow Elementary
an imprint of
Enslow Publishers, Inc.
40 Industrial Road
Box 398
Berkeley Heights, NJ 07922
USA
http://www.enslow.com

CONTENTS

WORDS TO KNOW

bonfire—A large outdoor fire. People had bonfires on Halloween to keep evil spirits away.

holiday—A day of celebration.

spirits—Ghosts.

jack-o'-lantern—A pumpkin with the insides removed. A light shines from inside to show the carved face.

3

AFTER DARK ON
OCTOBER 31

This is a time for fun! You dress up in a costume. You go trick or treating with friends. You get lots of candy and treats. It must be Halloween!

SPIRITS

Hundreds of years ago, people believed evil spirits came out on Halloween night. They put out food for the spirits. They wanted to keep them outside. They lit bonfires to scare them away.

SCARY
FACES

Children used to carve scary faces on turnips. They did this to scare away evil spirits. Now kids do this with pumpkins. They put candles in them. They are called **jack-o'-lanterns**.

COSTUMES

Today, kids wear costumes. They dress as ghosts and witches. Some are monsters and mummies. Some kids wear costumes that are not scary. They may be doctors or dancers.

TRICK OR TREATING

Kids also go from house to house. They knock on the door and say, "trick or treat!" They may get candy, snacks, or gum. Lots of children eat too many sweets that night!

PARADES AND PARTIES

Some towns have parades. Young people march in their costumes. There are also parties. Kids play games. They tell scary stories. They have candy, cupcakes, and punch.

HAUNTED FUN

Many people decorate their homes. Witches sit on the steps. Ghosts hang from the trees. Some kids go on haunted hayrides. They ride in a wagon. It is fun to be scared!

HALLOWEEN

HOLIDAY

Halloween is a night of fun for kids. Some say it is a kids' **holiday**. Hope your Halloween is spooky good!

GHOULISHLY GOOD HAND AND EYEBALL PUNCH

You and your friends will enjoy this scary fun party drink!

Here is what you will need:

- ❖ thin rubber glove (the type used in hospitals)
- ❖ red food coloring
- ❖ rubber band
- ❖ 2-liter bottle of cold, clear soda, such as ginger ale
- ❖ half gallon of lime sherbet
- ❖ 30 peeled grapes
- ❖ water and ice cubes

Do this the day before you make the punch:

- ❖ Fill the rubber glove with water.
- ❖ Add 5 drops of red food coloring to the water.
- ❖ Fasten the glove closed with the rubber band.
- ❖ Place the glove in the freezer for at least 15 hours.

Do this an hour before you want the punch:

- ❖ Leave the sherbet out until it softens and begins to melt.
- ❖ Place the softened sherbet in a large punch bowl.
- ❖ Pour the cold soda into the punch bowl.
- ❖ Stir until the sherbet is completely melted.
- ❖ Take the glove out of the freezer and gently pull the glove off the frozen hand form. Place the hand in the punch bowl. It will look like a floating bloody hand!
- ❖ Toss in the peeled grapes. They are the eyeballs.
- ❖ Add the ice cubes.

Enjoy your Ghoulishly Good Hand and Eyeball Punch!

LEARN MORE

BOOKS

Court, Rob. *How to Draw Halloween Things*. Mankato, Minn.: The Child's World, 2007.

Gillis, Jennifer Blizin. *Halloween*. Chicago: Heinemann, 2009.

Stevens, Kathryn. *Halloween Jack-o'-Lanterns*. Mankato, Minn.: The Child's World, 2010.

Trueit, Trudi Strain. *Halloween*. New York: Children's Press, 2007.

WEB SITES

PBS Kids: Happy Halloween

www.pbskids.org/halloween/

Halloween Coloring Pages

http://www.coloring-page.com/halloween.html

INDEX

Enslow Elementary, an imprint of Enslow Publishers, Inc.

Enslow Elementary® is a registered trademark of Enslow Publishers, Inc.

Copyright © 2012 by Elaine Landau

Library of Congress Cataloging-in-Publication Data

Landau, Elaine.
 What is Halloween? / by Elaine Landau.
  p. cm. — (I like holidays!)
 Includes index.
 Summary: "An introduction to Halloween with an easy activity"—Provided by publisher.
 ISBN 978-0-7660-3700-7
 1. Halloween. I. Title.
 GT4965.L35 2012
 394.2646—dc22

 2010039477

Paperback ISBN 978-1-59845-293-8

Printed in China

052011 Leo Paper Group, Heshan City, Guangdong, China

10 9 8 7 6 5 4 3 2 1

To Our Readers: We have done our best to make sure all Internet Addresses in this book were active and appropriate when we went to press. However, the author and the publisher have no control over and assume no liability for the material available on those Internet sites or on other Web sites they may link to. Any comments or suggestions can be sent by e-mail to comments@enslow.com or to the address on the back cover.

Photo Credits: © Banana Stock/PunchStock, pp. 13, 23; iStockphoto.com: © Carmen Martínez Banús, p. 4, © Sean Locke, p. 15; Photos.com, pp. 12, 20 (grapes); Shutterstock.com, pp. 1, 2, 3, 6, 7, 8, 9, 10, 11, 14, 16, 17, 18, 20.

Cover Photo: Shutterstock.com

Series Consultant:
Duncan R. Jamieson, PhD
Professor of History
Ashland University
Ashland, OH

Series Literacy Consultant:
Allan A. De Fina, PhD
Dean, College of Education
Professor of Literacy Education
New Jersey City University
Past President of the New Jersey
Reading Association